# INTRODUCTION:

If you've been roaming through the aisles of the local pet store checking out their selection of reptiles, wondering what lizard might be right for you, perhaps you should look no further than the leopard gecko. Leopard geckos are attractive lizards with mellow dispositions. They make a wonderful introduction to keeping reptiles as pets. They are easy to care for and require only a minimum of space. Leopard geckos are also readily available in almost any pet store that has a reptile department. Most leopard geckos are captive produced by private breeders rather than collected in the wild and imported into the country. Captive produced reptiles generally have fewer health issues, such as parasites or bacterial infections, and therefore make a better choice for the inexperienced keeper.

Leopard geckos originate from the dry deserts of Pakistan, India and Afghanistan. They are terrestrial geckos, who inhabit rocky outcroppings and are rarely seen climbing. They lack the sticky toe pads that arboreal (tree dwelling) Geckos have. The sticky toe pads are actually made up of millions of tiny hairs known as lamellae. This is what allows some geckos to walk up walls or hang upside down.

All geckos are members of the family *Gekkonidae* and leopard geckos are further classified into the subfamily *Eublepharinae*. All geckos in the subfamily *Eublepharinae* are unique in the gecko world in that they have eyelids. The name "leopard gecko" is known in the scientific community as *Eublepharis Macularius*. *Eublepharis* is the genus name and refers to the group of Geckos that have eyelids, and *Macularius* is the species name and means "spotted." Of the five known geckos in the genus *Eublepharis*, only the leopard gecko is available in the pet trade.

# TYPES OF LEOPARD GECKOS:

While all leopard geckos are members of the same species, they display an abundance of color and pattern variation that perhaps rivals that of all other lizards available in pet stores. With such a diversity of appearance, many refer to leopard geckos as the koi of the reptile market. This diversity of appearance is the result of selective captive breeding for color and pattern traits. The most common leopard geckos available in pet stores are considered to be the "High-Yellow" leopard geckos. They posess the name "High-Yellow" because they usually have a significantly smaller amount of dark spots than their cousins in the wild.

*Leopard geckos in their native habitat frequently have numerous spots of dark pigmentation.*

*Geckos such as these may be found at a store near you.*

There are a great deal of pattern variations in leopard geckos, from distinct bands to jungle patterns and even specks of tangerine in the tail.

*Patternless Leopard Gecko*

Another leopard gecko readily found in pet stores is the patternless variation. These geckos get their pattern, or lack thereof, from a recessive gene.

All of the geckos described thus far are commonly found in pet stores for between $50-$100, but no section entitled "Types of Leopard Geckos" would be complete without a look at some of the living works of art being produced through selective leopard gecko breeding.

*A wide variety of beautiful leopard geckos can be found through private breeders and specialty stores.*

As one might guess, more exotic means more expensive. For those looking for something unique, leopard geckos like the ones above are easily purchased from commercial breeders or over the internet for $125 and up. Simply type "leopard gecko" in your favorite search engine, and you're sure to find abundant amounts of information.

# IS A LEOPARD GECKO THE RIGHT PET FOR YOU?

A leopard gecko is the perfect pet lizard for a young child or a grade school classroom. Their small space requirements also make them ideal for places where room is limited, such as an apartment or dormroom. Leopard geckos are also relatively inexpensive to set-up and maintain, so they make a good choice for the reptile fan on a budget. A basic set-up, including the animal, and which will be sufficient for the animal's ENTIRE lifetime, should cost no more than $200.

Leopard geckos are small yet sturdy lizards growing as large as 10 inches (25.4 CM). While they are solid full figured animals, they are gentle and not intimidating. Leopard geckos will readily tame down with handling and are sturdy enough for young children to interact with.

Like all reptiles, leopard geckos do not affect people with allergies as dogs and cats do, making them perfect pets for these individuals.

Leopard geckos are long-lived lizards, some having been reported to live over 30 years in captivity, so your new baby leopard gecko may be passed down a generation.

# SELECTING A HEALTHY ANIMAL:

An unhealthy leopard gecko is fairly easy to spot. By following some basic guidelines, you should walk away with a healthy animal.

First, never buy a leopard gecko that doesn't have a tail that's noticeably fatter and wider than its hips, which should also appear full with no visible bones. Leopard geckos with very thin tails often perish, even in the most experienced keeper's hands.

*This gecko is thin and dehydrated. Do not purchase a gecko that shows similar symptoms.*

Watch out for geckos that seem to have loose flaps of skin or are missing toes, these are usually signs of malnutrition and improper husbandry.

Your gecko should appear fat and healthy. Health problems in adults and sub-adults are easier to spot than in juvenile animals. An adult or sub-adult leopard gecko should feel quite solid in your hand and appear full bodied with a broad, bulging tail.

Remember, if purchasing a pair of geckos, you should buy a male and a female or two females. Male leopard geckos are very territorial and may injure each other as a result of combat when housed together.

Geckos with missing or re-generated tails are sometimes offered for sale, often at a discounted price from their perfect cage mates. There is nothing permanently wrong with these geckos. Lost tails will grow back, but they will lose their distinct ridging, and may be a bit misshapen. Some re-grown tails can be more vibrantly colored too.

Leopard geckos can be easily sexed by looking at their vents, located on the underside of their bellies where their back legs meet the body. Male geckos will have a V-shaped row of enlarged pre-anal pores stretched along the legs from each side of the vent. Females still have these pores but they are significantly less pronounced. Leopard geckos can be difficult to sex until they are at least 4-6 months of age. Leopard geckos are one of the few geckos where sex can be determined by incubation temperature, so breeders may already know the sex of leopard geckos while still in the egg!

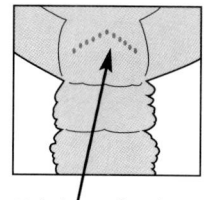

*Male leopard geckos have a v-shaped row of enlarged pre-anal pores.*

When purchasing a leopard gecko, look for an animal that's alert and active with wide, attentive eyes. Ask to hold the animal, it should feel solid and be alert. Inspect the animal's skin to see if there's any scarring from possible cage mate bullies. Inspect the mouth area to be sure it is clean and intact with no sign of rot or damage. Also check the animal's vent and underside. It should be clean with no sign of fecal residue. Make sure the animal has all its toes and that no dried shed is attached anywhere, especially the toe area.

# HOUSING:

*A basic set up for leopard geckos*

Leopard geckos are one of the easiest lizards to set up and care for, so long as all the necessities are provided. Leopard geckos require a fairly small amount of space to live comfortably. A ten-gallon (or

15 gallon "breeder") tank is suitable housing for a single leopard gecko for life. A twenty gallon tank would work for up to three geckos. "Breeder" style, or short tanks, make great enclosures for leopard geckos as they are usually about 6 inches shorter than a standard size tank, but also six inches deeper, providing more surface area for the geckos to live in. The lack of headroom won't bother your geckos as they spend almost all of their time on the ground.

Sand, such as Zoo Med's Repti Sand™ or Vita Sand, is an appropriate substrate for leopard geckos. A layer about 2 inches deep should be provided across the entire floor of the enclosure.

There should be a hiding spot on both the warm and cool sides of the enclosure to help your new gecko feel safe and secure in their new home.

Shallow bowls should be provided for food and water. The author uses and recommends Zoo Med's Small Repti Rock™ Water and Food Dishes, as they are the perfect depth for leopard geckos to get in and out of easily.

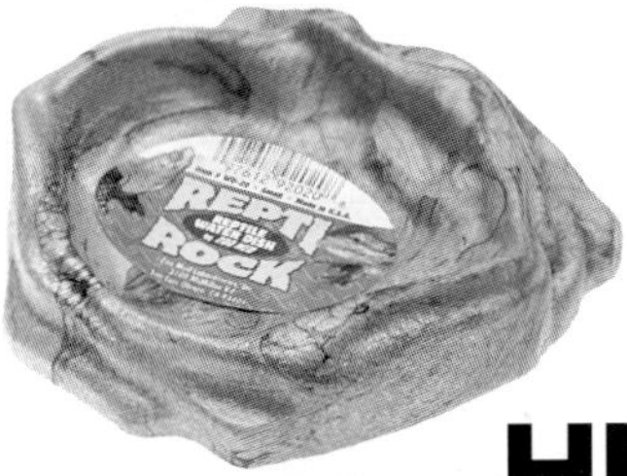

*Zoo Med's Repti Sand™*

*Zoo Med's Vita Sand™*

*Zoo Med's Repti Rock™ Water Dish*

*Zoo Med's Repti Rock™ Food Dish*

## HEATING

Like all reptiles, leopard geckos are ectothermic, meaning they derive their body heat through external sources. Reptiles cannot internally regulate their blood temperature, and must seek out warm areas to heat their blood. This is why giving your new pet a warm home is of paramount importance.

Your Gecko's enclosure should be about 85°F (29°C) on the warm side and as low as 75°F (24°C) on the cool side, a 5°F drop (2°C) in temperature is acceptable during nighttime hours, however, the hiding spot on the warm side should never drop below 80°F (27°C). Since leopard geckos rely on variable outside temperatures in order to regulate their own body temperature, a range or gradient of temperatures should be provided.

The tank may be heated with a heat pad, such as Zoo Med's ReptiTherm UTH™. Place the heat pad on one side of the tank thus creating a warm and a cool side. This thermal gradient allows the geckos to self regulate their heat and remain as comfortable as possible.

Daytime overhead heating should also be provided in larger cages. A daylight flood bulb, such as Zoo Med's Daylight Blue Bulb™, is a good choice. The bulb should stay on for 12-14 hours during the day, and the heating pad should be left on 24 hours for nighttime heating, as well. Be sure to position the heating lamp on the warm side, but not directly above the heating pad. Putting the daytime bulb on a timer makes keeping your geckos warm an easy and convenient task.

Whenever using heating devices in a reptile enclosure it's a good idea to have them hooked up to a thermostat, such as Zoo Med's ReptiTemp 500R™. A thermostat will allow you to control the maximum temperature within your pet's enclosure. You should always buy a thermostat with a remote sensor probe. This allows the thermostat to be placed outside the enclosure while the probe is fed inside the tank. By placing the thermostat's probe on the warm side of the enclosure and adjusting the heat to about 86°F (30°C), you can be away at work knowing that the thermostat will shut off any heating devices in your pet's enclosure, should it become too hot.

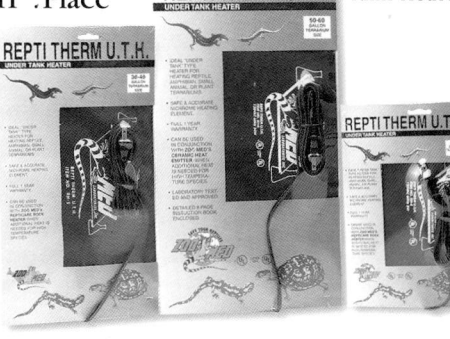

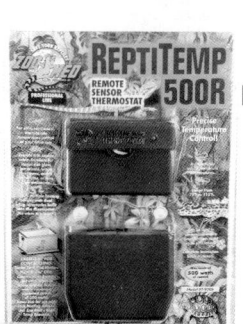

## Shed box:

Leopard geckos come from a dry desert environment, but require a humid area to aid in shedding their skin. While providing humidity, it's important to ensure most of your gecko's environment remains dry. Too much humidity in your gecko's

*A small plastic container makes a great shed box.*

**Zoo Med's Eco Earth™**

environment can cause a respiratory infection in your animal. To keep the humidity in one part of the enclosure high while the rest remains dry, a small plastic container should be used. For a single gecko, choose a sandwich-sized container. Fill the container half way with sphagnum moss or a coconut bedding, such as Zoo Med's Eco Earth™. Cut a hole in the lid of the plastic container that's just large enough for the gecko to easily fit through. This is now your shed box. Place the shed box on the cool end, or near the middle of the enclosure, and keep the moss moist, but not wet.

## Vivaria:

We have gone over all that is necessary for a basic set up for your geckos, which doesn't necessarily make for the most breathtaking display. To go a step further and make an attempt at replicating their natural environment, a vivaria, or naturalistic display, can be created. Leopard geckos make great vivaria subjects; since they are relatively small they don't tend to "rough-up" plants in the enclosure like other

*Leopard geckos make great vivarium subjects!*

lizards may.

The first step in creating a beautiful display is hiding the shed box. Stacking some rocks in the rear of the enclosure to create a "cubby" will camouflage the shed box and easily solves this problem. Be sure to design the "cubby" so that it allows you easy access to the shed box for misting. Placing a plant in front of the rock cubby will further hide the shed box and beautify the enclosure. Plants such as Sanseveria and Aloe make good choices for desert vivaria as they grow slowly, can be liberally trimmed, and have low light requirements.

**Zoo Med's Reptisun 2.0™**

To ensure that your geckos are safe from toxicity, any plants added to the vivaria should be planted in organic soil with no pearlite. Keeping the plants in small plastic pots which you can bury in the sand, makes maintenance of your vivaria a bit easier.

When keeping plants, the addition of full spectrum lighting such as Zoo Med's Reptisun 2.0™, is highly recommended. Full spectrum lighting will help replicate sunlight for the plants and the geckos, and will also make your vivaria well lit for your viewing pleasure.

If succulents or cacti are to be added, further research is recommended, and a group of two or more full spectrum fluorescent lights will be required.

# FOOD

Leopard geckos are insectivorous lizards and should be fed a diet of crickets and worms.

Luckily these insects are easily found at most any pet store that has a reptile department. Adult geckos should be offered as much food as they will eat at least once every three days. Sub-adult and juvenile geckos should eat to their content at least 5 days a week.

## Live food:

Crickets and worms are great food sources that are commonly stocked at pet stores. When feeding crickets a good rule of thumb is to only offer crickets that are no larger then the width of your geckos head. Two-week old crickets are recommended for juvenile and sub adult geckos, and four week old crickets are recommended for adults. Try to offer your geckos a mix of crickets and various worms. King and super mealworms make great offerings for your adult geckos. Other worms, such as butterworms or silkworms, may be offered as well. These worms are high in fat and should not be a sole food item for your gecko. Mini mealworms are a favorite of newly hatched and juvenile geckos.

Zoo Med's Can O' Crickets™ and Can O' Worms™

## Commercial diets:

Of the various commercial diets on the market, the author recommends Zoo Med's Can O' Crickets™ and Can O' Worms™. These diets contain retorted (i.e.: cooked in the can) insects that may be used as a complete replacement of live food. Feed these in the same frequency you offer live food. Place them in a shallow bowl in the enclosure. It helps to always place the bowl in the same location each time. Your gecko may need training time to adjust to eating a non-live food. Try enticing them towards the food bowl by offering a retorted insect on tongs, such as Zoo Med's Feeding Tongs™.

### Vitamin and Mineral Supplements:

A vitamin and mineral supplement, such as Zoo Med's Reptivite™, must be offered as part of the weekly feeding schedule. To add the vitamin and mineral powder to the diet, put a single helping of crickets or worms (live or retorted) in a small plastic bag. Add about one quarter of a teaspoon of supplement powder to the bag, and shake. This should leave the insects "dusted" and ready for feeding. Adult leopard geckos should have their food dusted about once per week. Sub-adult and juvenile Leopard geckos should have their food dusted twice weekly.

**Zoo Med's Feeding Tongs™**

# BEHAVIOR

### Shedding:

Your leopard gecko will periodically shed, when doing so you will notice they spend a fair amount of time in their shed box and may even sleep there. When your gecko is shedding, its colors will seem to fade as its outer layer of skin becomes loose. Your gecko will now grab hold of a piece of the shed and begin tugging on it consuming the shed as it pulls it off. The shed box needs to stay moist to ensure that shedding is a smooth process and that your gecko is able to shed all of its skin easily. One of the most commonly seen problems with captive kept leopard geckos is an inability to properly shed the old skin off of their toes. If this skin isn't removed it can restrict blood flow to the toe and the toe may simply fall off in time. Tweezers are helpful when assisting your gecko in shedding the skin in these areas.

**Zoo Med's Reptivite™**

### Hunting:
Leopard geckos are avid hunters and will put on a show whenever live crickets are placed into the enclosure. The geckos will stalk the crickets shaking their tails before they pounce. They are effective hunters and hearty eaters. Although leopard geckos are nocturnal, they will frequently eat by day when food is offered.

### Hiding:
Leopard geckos are nocturnal, spending most of their day in hiding, venturing out at night to hunt and frolic. By hiding, leopard geckos feel more secure from predators while they are sleeping.

### Mating:
Leopard gecko mating rituals are fairly straightforward. The male will court the female by chasing her around the enclosure and nipping at her tail. Once the female is caught, the male will mount her and grab hold with a bite to the neck or head. He will then move his tail below hers to gain access to her vent and begin copulation. Biting is a normal part of mating behavior for leopard geckos, but if the ritual becomes too violent, or the female is being damaged by the male's advances, the two animals should be separated for a short period. The female may be later introduced to the male's cage for supervised visits.

### Handling your pet:
Your new gecko may be a bit squeamish and hard to handle at first, but in a fairly short amount of time it will become a calm, easy to handle creature. It has been the author's experience that male geckos tame down more quickly than females, while both become easy to handle in a short amount of time. These geckos are very reluctant to bite, but may, just as any animal would, if they feel sufficiently threatened. While handling your gecko, it is important not to apply too much pressure to its tail, and never grab your gecko by the tail alone. Leopard geckos will drop their tails as part of their defensive strategy to escape predators. By

dropping their tails and quickly running away, they hope to distract the predator and get away to live another day. Luckily their tails will regenerate.

When handling your gecko, try to stick out your palm and get it to crawl onto your hand. If this fails you can pick up your gecko by grasping it firmly on its body behind its front legs. You may have to "stalk and pounce" with your hand to catch the gecko, but practice will make perfect. Put the gecko on your outstretched palm and let it crawl around. Chances are your new pet will lick you to see what you taste like, I don't recommend licking him back, as he probably won't respond well. Playing with your leopard gecko and petting his bumpy skin is a joy, but shouldn't be overdone as it may cause undue stress on the animal.

# HEALTH:

While leopard geckos are hardy lizards with minimal care requirements, they can still fall prey to illness and disease. Your leopard gecko's appearance and behavior are the best indicators of their health.

### Malnutrition:

A malnourished gecko will appear thin with skin folds, and a tail that simply goes to a point from the hips with no bulge (see page 6). Malnourished geckos will also lose color and appear muted or light. Depending on the severity of the malnourishment, the gecko may not be able to live through rehabilitation. A regiment of fatty foods, such as silkworms, butterworms, or wax worms, supplemented with a vitamin powder every other feeding, is recommended. A malnourished gecko may also have some illnesses related to supplementation.

### Supplementation issues:

An animal that has hypo-vitaminosis (A lack of Vitamin A) can lose its color and sometimes refuse to eat. Similar symptoms are found with hyper calcification (too much calcium). Because of the

# BREEDING A PAIR OF LEOPARD GECKOS:

If you have male and female leopard geckos living together, there is very good chance they will mate. Taking care of the eggs and hatching out the young is a wonderful experience that is highly recommended. Breeding a pair of leopard geckos also makes a great classroom experience or science project. If your female leopard gecko is gravid (carrying eggs) she will have a pair of easily seen eggs on the lower part of her underbelly. Once you notice this, the shed box should be moved onto the warm side of the enclosure, but not under any over-head heating. In a few weeks she will most likely lay her eggs in the moist soil. Now comes the incubation period. In order to incubate the eggs they must remain in moist soil at temperatures ranging from 80° to 90°F (27°-30°C). In order to accomplish this, an inexpensive chicken style incubator may be purchased. A simpler, but less predictable method is to simply keep the eggs in a small container, like a deli cup, on the warm side of the enclosure. The lid of the container should have 4-6 small sized holes for ventilation. Fill the deli cup halfway with a material such as vermiculite or coconut bedding that is moist but not wet. About a 50:50 water to filler material ratio by weight is recommended. The eggs (leopard geckos generally lay 2 eggs) should be placed so they are halfway in the soil, be very careful not to rotate the eggs in any way while moving them! The egg bin should be checked regularly to ensure that the proper moisture levels are maintained. To add moisture, a mister may be used on the stream setting. Mist on the edges of the container making sure not to spray directly on the eggs. In 45 to 60 days, baby leopard geckos should start hatching. Place the juvenile geckos in a smaller version of your adult's setup, complete with a thermal gradient, hide spot, shed box, and water bowl. Juvenile leopard geckos need small food items offered at least 6 days a week, and should be fed as much as they will eat. Don't worry if your newborn gecko doesn't eat for the first several days, many juveniles don't eat until after their first shed, living off of the yolk sac they had in the egg.

To learn more about breeding your leopard geckos check out some of the books on my recommended reading list.

## SUMMARY

We hope through reading this book you have gained the knowledge needed to provide good basic care to your new leopard gecko, and have a happy and healthy pet that you will enjoy.

We're sure you will find that leopard geckos are easy to care for and have interesting personalities. It would make us proud to know that these little geckos have given you the kind of joy they give us.

### Recommended Reading:

**The Leopard Gecko Manual**
*By Philippe de Vosjoli, Brian Viets,*
*Ron Tremper, and Roger Klingenberg, DVM*
*Published by Advanced Vivarium Systems*

**The Leopard Gecko:**
**An Owners Guide To A Happy Healthy Pet**
*By Lyle Puente*
*Published by Hungry Minds, Inc.*

**Design and maintenance of Desert Vivaria**
*By Philippe deVosjoli*
*Published by Advanced Vivarium Systems*

# MAINTENANCE CHECKLIST:

## Daily:
Clean and fill water bowls
Clean and fill food bowl, if one is used
Clean up any uneaten food on substrate

## Weekly:
- Give the cage a thorough inspection, checking to make sure substrate and cage décor are free of uneaten food, or any sort of debris.
- Sterilize all dishes or bowls.
- Make sure there are proper moisture levels in the shed box.
- Replace shed box filler material if needed. (replace monthly regardless)

## Feeding and supplementation schedule:

### Juvenile and sub-adult animals:
- Offer food at least 5 times weekly.
- Supplement with a vitamin/mineral powder twice weekly.

### Adult animals:
- Offer food at least 3 times weekly.
- Supplement with a vitamin/mineral powder once weekly.

# THE PHI DELTA KAPPA
## GALLUP POLLS
### OF
## ATTITUDES TOWARD EDUCATION
## 1969-1984
### A TOPICAL SUMMARY

STANLEY M. ELAM, EDITOR

Ministry of Education, Ontario
Information Centre, 13th Floor,
Mowat Block, Queen's Park,
Toronto, Ont.　　M7A 1L2

Cover design by Kathe Swann

Library of Congress Catalog Card Number 84-61700
ISBN 0-87367-792-7
Copyright © 1984 by Phi Delta Kappa
Bloomington, Indiana